Chris Sykes

Having an Osprey About the House

MAGPIE PRESS

First published 2001 by Magpie Press
26 Ambassador Court, Leamington Spa,
Warwickshire CV32 6JF
e-mail magpiepoetry@aol.com

ISBN 0 9523449 5 5

A CIP catalogue record for this book is available from
the British Library.

Printed and bound in Great Britain by
Warwick Printing Company, Warwick

for my mother

Acknowledgements

Thanks to the editors of the following, in which some of these poems first appeared: *Acumen, The Cricketer International, Envoi, First Time, The Magazine, The Rialto, Rivet, Spokes, Staple.*

Also *The Experience of Poetry*, Open College of the Arts, and *The Spirit of Cricket*, Faber and Faber.

Cover design by Ralph Lillford

Contents

15 Childhood Poems

Having an Osprey About the House

Salt Spray

Don't tell me why
birds fly by,
why the insect
likes the flower,

how the blue
becomes the sky
or how a minute
forms an hour.

Don't tell me what
bird song means
or the call of the
hump-backed whale.

Truth is just
the salt spray
plunged in the
dolphin's tail.

Lunacy

Birds lived in water in winter, on the skin
of the moon, people once thought. The Seas
of Crisis and Tranquillity, the Ocean of Storms,
the Lake of Dreams, all teeming with birds.
The Bays of Rainbow and of Dew, worlds
of birds too. Deep bowls of blue water

with birds in. Yet the moon's seas have no water
science tells us. No vibrations disturb its skin,
there's no sound, even of wings. The moon world
has only shadowed dust plains as its seas,
and nights cold as liquid air mean no birds
could survive on a dead globe of dust storms.

Yet, standing on a beach in a winter storm,
I saw the shape of wing tips breaking water
up on the moon; a small speckle of birds
at first on its pearly white skin;
then more rising up from those deep lunar seas,
trailing flight over that world.

Birdless winter blizzards held our world
but up there in the cloud and light storms
thermal currents of birds were threading the Seas
of Nectar and Serenity. Buzzards, shearwaters,
barnacle geese flaking the moon's skin.
In their wake eddies of other birds –

flycatchers, blackcaps, soaring blackbirds,
starlings, thrushes, swallows. This world
held me and the more I looked up at its skin
the more I saw what the scientists missed; storms
of birds flown from our dreams, flocks of water
birds poised in flight over the moon seas.

I watched them rise in one flock from those seas,
the thrumbling, uprushing, open-winged birds.
Having kept for years to the moon's silvery waters,
burnished and brightened by that world
they were readying to fly back in a new storm
of wings across space's vast starlit skin

to our seas. And they're coming back to our world,
birds and birds, flooding through the star-storms -
moon water to feather again our dreaming skins.

A Falling Leaf

That the most can be the least,
that a leaf can be a flower,
that a squirrel can be a thief,
and a falling leaf an hour.

That a root can be a snake,
the ivy leaf an adder's tongue
and bird song sit so silent
in the moment that it's sung.

That the dew can be so white,
and the silence of a fly
can be the tenderness of night
as it draws the evening by.

A Night Like This

It will be a night like this,
bird spinning its song in a thicket,
the stars all slipped to earth,
slow along the roads.

It will be a night like this -
swollen river brown with rain
and meadow mirrors
spread across the grass

for the swans to float in.
It will be a night like this,
stone bodies stood together,

the duck and wind refrain,
when we stand here listening;
listening to it all again.

Crossing Derwent Water

1. *Skiddaw*

Saddleback, Grisedale Pike,
Skiddaw. Ridge-backs
rising through the mist,
prehistoric creatures

the earth brought to rest
millennia ago. They lay
on their slumbering bellies
while human centuries passed.

Farmers laid down necklaces
of drystone walls, brought sheep
to graze the folds of new-grown
grass and moss, even while

they knew the whale-backs would
one day uproot themselves,
plunge into the fathoms of the lakes,
on their hidden rudders,

iron-rock powering them down
from where they came,
leaving human cities drowning
in an avalanche of rain.

2. *Fell Falling*

Lakeland morning mist.
Great Sca Fell and Lonscale Fell
are only cavities of earth

rising into the sky to meet
the falling sound of air.
From heather and furze

the eagle, bloody with sheep,
the world within its eye,
shrieks the racing wind.

3. *Lakeland Morning*

Crossing Derwent Water
no other moment lives
so temporal and eternal

as this, no other sound
dips into what is but the quiet
boat, and the reflection

on the lake of red squirrels
in the conifers and beech.
The rain in whispering oak.

Having an Osprey About the House

Shouting at the end of the hall,
someone arriving, brushing down the dog
and laughing at wild, insatiable love.
Then voices, glasses and wine;

click of knife on plate,
the crumbly gossiping of bread rolls;
'I like to have my fish and eat it.'
Here the imprecise edges of words brush

each other. Outside, through the glass,
the decked larkspur and delphinium
sway like the juice of a July afternoon
distilled in the sky's night bowl.

Close to the ceiling the osprey hangs
silently moving blue surface shadows
with its wide spread wings, out
hunting the skim of the glassy Loch

choosing the moment to enter the cool,
and dragged, ever deeper down
into the thrashes of the numbed load.
He fights up again into the air,

talons hooked in shaking scale-silver,
plunging his wings free and lifting himself
out over the table, through the dazed glitter
of eyes, out over the blue blossom globe.

Suburban Dream

I am a dream of poems
with light in, like lobster pots
held against the sun
and pouring full of holes,

or like houses full of rooms
to wander in, sofas to lie on,
chairs to sink into,
the window open

and curtains moving,
music flapping
in and out of idle air,
a bell that rings,

the sound of springs,
cricket bat, photograph,
red-velvet cushion on a chair,
unmade beds, tousled heads,

arms and legs, piles of clothes,
and outside, children laughing
in the garden, sleek with water
from a hose.

Geisha Fish

The noise of fish
as they pop up to breathe,
leaving their ripples
where they rose,
in concentric circles
touching one another
in the stream.

Lips of a hundred geishas
glossy beneath umbrellas
threading through
a Tokyo street;
legs in kimonos
smooth and silver
and so slim.

Nowhere More Than This

It is written
soundlessly in air
as the sky draws
a humming cloth
over all the houses'
white facades

before it slips to earth
in the begonia beds
pampas grass and cedar,
in the young girl
doing head-rolls,

handstands and cartwheels
in red trousers
for her father
applauding on the long,
flat stretch of mown

and manicured grass;
it is written soundlessly
in air in the shouts the boys
in turbans, playing
interracial polo

off the backs of bikes,
let drift across the river,
road and grass that this
is the undetermined
and eternal hour.

The Overhanging Rose

Say I am two sticks rubbed with coal
who are the teachers of my heart and soul?
What insubstantiality of flame dances between
the two sticks in the charred cleft, unseen?

Truth, so far as I can understand,
is mine, rises from my own hand.
If all I've read and all I've lived is proof
to the historian of time, myself, that I am truth,

then doubt softens into a summer's day that carries
an evening in through windows full of gooseberries
shining in white bowls. While I toe and heel
the hairy globes and concoct a meal

of fish and mushrooms and milk and thyme
my body feels gently warmed, as by a climb
up a steep yet gentle hill in summer rain.
I smell water on my hands. I smell them now again.

I am made of water. My skin is pores of water.
And I am one who sometimes dreams himself a daughter,
washing clothes and folding clothes
I'll hang them where they brush the overhanging rose.

The Time It Takes

In the time it takes to read these words
a tropical rain forest will be consumed.
One hundred acres of trees and birds

laid into wreaths of smoke. Curling upward
smoke from a pyre, a death foredoomed
in the time it takes to read these words.

Ahead of the smoke fly the mynah birds
out of the air that itself will assume
one hundred acres of trees and birds.

The fingers of smoke claw, unperturbed,
catching the birds and trees of their plumes.
In the time it takes to read these words

they fly on flame, blackened and unfurred,
the songbird, lyre-bird, brightly costumed.
One hundred acres of trees and birds

drifting in air like thoughts that have occurred
out of a book, like cigarette smoke in a room,
in the time it takes to read these words –
one hundred acres of trees and birds.

Venezia 1608

'La studio della pittura é faticoso, a sempre si fa il mare maggiore.'
attributed to Tintoretto

Century of alchemy; anatomists pared the bones
and brains of hares, peeled the human womb
of muscle and skin to probe the bud of life thought within.
Alive to his Masters, Tintoretto, Veronese, Tiziano Vecelli,

he made a book of hands – all the merchants, bankers,
cardinals and courtesans with dirty fingernails
above the stink of the Ponte di Rialto. From among
the market stalls of Campo di Santa Maria Formosa

he drew hands stinking of fungi. At Quay San Marco
the hands of dark gondoliers, fishmongers' hands sticky
with gutted mess, cooks' fingers slimy with octopus
and squid. Behind sun-white blinds in Piazza di San Marco

there were musicians fingering mandolins golden as chicken
breasts. He studied the Signore de Venezia shaking hands
with foreign diplomats, behind them their informers' hands
whispering of money and he caught the dangerous

hands of their black-eyed daughters and wives. Going
home through people foul with sweat and unwashed
clothes, through cut ditches and stagnant canals, past
dank stairwells of mouldering wood, water undulating

like moonlight on a marble floor and the full moon
rising out of the sea to tremble on domes and cupolas,
he moved, thrilled. Till, locked with the Jews behind
iron gates, dusk to dawn, in the Ghetto Vecchio,

in an old house eaten by the sea, sweating
with the Countess Falco above summer's foetid streets
when her gondola had come for him, he suddenly knew
he could not stare steel-eyed into the heat of it all

and still keep his sight. That the artist could not cut a smell
in half to try and understand. And at Candelmas, gold
mosaics flickering overhead, soldiers frosted in armour
at the door, while the Doge's hands raised a flagon of wine

and the ranks of Christian Signore, their daughters
and wives sang for victory against the Turk, outside,
Odoardo Fialetti cupped his hands like her warm white
thighs around his face to know again the smell of her

hotness arcing above him in bed. And her grip became
eagle talons clawing the wound into his brain, where four
centuries later it was found by me, speared on terra rossa,
still screaming like a delirious rabbit heart in pain.

14 Preludes

i.
Younger, in odd clothes,
and with its hair different,
the past always smells
funny, looks innocent.

ii.
Life lives us out
and leaves us emptied
before we know anything
of its game.
(There is no game)

iii.
Sadness is a serious illness
because it can be enjoyed.

iv.
Ducks, like happy acrobats,
fly into the air
they know will always wait
to catch them there.

v.
Whatever we are
we must learn to be.

vi.
In the long black night
we are becalmed ships
suckled by the old long boats -
fear, penance, innocence.

vii
When they come to again
my thoughts always surprise me
by not being where they were
put down.

viii.
Sleep empties memory
so it can be filled again.

ix.
Now I feel
like a wicker garden chair
the frost has sat
long hours in.

x.
I should like the power
to unite the smile
I can adopt later
with the moment of pain.

xi.
Even quickening my pace
through mud, I can't shake off
grey footprints
that run after me.

xii.
When I speak
I sometimes say things.

xiii.
I am a clown in big shoes:
every time I walk towards something
I kick it away from me.
I can only laugh.

xiv.
Though now I know too
another thing of grief.
It grows into itself;
into bones, into mouths,
into eyes, into smiles;
and quietly desists.

The Thief

The thrush is not free in its feathers,
gold not free in its leaf,
the flower is not free in white heather,
the owner of all is a thief.

Oak trees are not free in the earth,
corn not free in its sheaf,
birth is not free giving birth,
the owner of all is a thief.

Clouds are not free in the air,
foam not free in a reef,
the rain is not free anywhere,
the owner of all is a thief.

A salmon is not free in its leap,
love not free on the flyleaf,
the mind is not free in its sleep,
the owner of all is a thief.

The river is not free in its water,
sadness not free in its grief,
a mother not free in her daughter,
the owner of all is a thief.

The Convolvulus of Time

Stone church on its knees in grass.
Anglican dead plaited together,
bone-cages woven into saffron tapestries
of blood-dock and bearded dead nettle.

In a skein of grey Suffolk rain,
words interred deep in stone;
'In Memory of Christopher Cumfell.'
'Here Lie The Mortal Remains

of Esther Neade and Rose Jane Neade.'
'To Those Who Gave Their Lives.'
'Emma, beloved wife of Thomas Harwood.'
'Isabella Dickinson.' 'William Webb'.

Summer evenings have skimmed like bats
over the long grass, and the stone heads
loll on one another like aged friends,
as young swimmers cross high-banks now

to and from the same river: Carol and Anne,
Julie and Mike, strawberry white skin,
boozy beer-breath and laughter.
Bare backed and bare-shouldered,

water-smacked hair, gleaming bare skin
they toss up their laurel laughs
against shadows of blackthorn and bramble,
ivy and elder. Make friends with the clover.

The Other Woman

'The softness of your skin against my breasts,
your mouth full of kisses. My God!' the letter said,
'Come tonight, I'll wear my little black lycra dress.'
She saw it with an awful, unrelenting dread,

at the bottom of the drawer on his side of the bed.
'I'm lying here dreaming of you, totally undressed.
Without you I'm nothing. I breathe but I am dead.
The softness of your skin against my breasts.

It's wonderful to fall asleep in your arms. My sweetest
one, you are my life.' The deadness in her spread;
a love letter to her husband from a woman quite possessed.
'Your mouth full of kisses. My God!' the letter said,

and more of flesh's wonder she left painfully unread.
She didn't need to name her, didn't need to guess.
She recognised the hand. She feared what lay ahead.
'Come tonight, I'll wear my little black lycra dress.'

A monument of loss these discovered words expressed.
Through the fleeing years all their love had fled.
By time, the great possessor, they lay unpossessed.
She saw it with an awful, unrelenting dread.

Their world of hope the gathered world had blessed,
the glowing rush of paradise to flesh. Instead,
there was no more terrible betrayal she could confess
once she saw the words with which she'd once garlanded
the softness of his skin, against her breasts.

Rivals

And when the snake has been born of the owl
that out of flight into earth comes to rest
then both the killer and victim who prowl

the earth will wonder who earth loves the best.
Think of owl entering the belly of snake
bearing its airy killings like a nest.

And snake speared in its cold head, on a wake
of its own devoured dead. Slitherer of grass,
thought of stone, grieving grief in a skin-flake.

So the earth grows out of the air's thin glass
to know itself in its trophies of dead,
all the lost bodies of creatures that pass.

The night of kindness to which cruelty's led,
killer and victim inhabiting one head.

Gender-Talk

'The designation of certain forms in grammar or prosody as "masculine" or "feminine" does not mean that these forms have anything to do with sex, but is a purely formal usage of nomenclature. Usually the designation masculine is given to the so-called strong concept, and feminine to the weak.'

(The Poet's Manual and Rhyming Dictionary)

The masculine rhyme will strengthen the line
where the feminine rhyme brings weakness.
In English the roles have long been assigned.
The feminine offers a sweet indirectness,

sometimes it is strongest, sometimes weakest,
but where the masculine gives bite to the text
the feminine will instead offer softness.
What I'm saying has nothing to do with sex.

It applies only in line-endings in rhyme
where it's masculine to end on a syllable of stress,
such as bed, war, hope, kill, love, dove, divine;
and feminine to offer a supple contour of supineness.

Feminine rhyme, in a sense, clothes or dresses
the masculine body. If the masculine, in this context,
is God the feminine is revealed of Godliness.
What I'm saying has nothing to do with sex.

I speak of sameness and difference that combine
in a world of words that, if it cares how to be honest,
knows the moon can suck its own shadow in sunshine.
As light shades dark and strength possesses weakness

24

if the masculine is great the feminine has greatness.
If the masculine can remain genuflexed
beneath arms that bless, it is the feminine that blesses.
What I'm saying has nothing to do with sex.

It is the English language that I address,
that blood-soaked quilt, that complex
interlocking organism of male and femaleness.
What I'm saying has everything to do with sex.

On Upsetting a Friend

Someday I'll speak no wrong,
a missel-thrush in song.
Someday I'll have the mind
of someone who is only kind.

Someday I'll be neither cruel nor bad,
I'll make everyone happy and not sad.
Someday I'll live not out of greed,
when all good things in me are freed.

Someday I'll make no mistakes,
from dawn to dusk as each day breaks,
someday when I wake instead
tongueless, deaf, blind and dead.

Gifts

White geranium in the glass,
sunlight varnishing the wooden floor,
blue glaze in the china bowl.

It is as if I begin
for the first time once more
to know it all.

Forgiving

Be as the broken paeony
flower.

Hadlee's Victim

Hadlee in, fast beneath
the high arc of his arm,
the ball delivered from his palm.

Then, that soft, sweet click,
and pause, as though a pin's
been pushed in air –

a gap closed over by applause.
Hadlee fluid, Gatting hurried,
middle stump knocked back,

the bail sent 20 yards behind
where umpire 'Dickie' Bird
walks to fetch it, shaking his head.

He straightens the stump,
knocked askew, so play,
when ready, can resume.

And the England captain trails off
past Father Time on the main stand
who, sickle on his shoulder

takes the bails off, and,
at the same time puts them on,
walks towards the shaded portraits
of the Long Room, his bat,

the drooping of his back
in the verdant shadows
of the pavilion now,
through the gate and up the steps.

Ripples

We are sitting with wine and tea by the river.
The tall brown teazles nod. You're reading a book.
I'm drawing you. A slow wind stirs the silver
willow leaves. Two riders on horseback look.

Their horses plunge the sunlit water one by one,
thrashing the surface with their bellies as they wade.
They leave in our eyes a glittery sense of going on.
We leave in theirs, perhaps, a sense of shade.

Meadowsweet

We have found a place to go.
We have found a place to walk,
where the river passes still and slow
going round the tiny island forks.

We have found a place to walk,
waist high in oats and wheat,
going round the tiny island forks
in all the banks of meadowsweet.

Waist high in oats and wheat,
where the river passes still and slow,
in all the banks of meadowsweet
we have found a place to go.

Luscious Couplets

i
Pale orchid lips of Himalayan Balsam,
dark with tonguing scent and thrum.

White dead nettle, honeyed lips
where the black bee dips.

Blue-bottles, hairy horse-flies,
conjoined turquoise dragon-flies.

Bay Willow, Meadow Cranesbill
luscious, mounding day to fill.

ii
Dry river banks of last year's oats,
plunged by the prows of wooden boats.

Ice on the frozen fields is glass,
massive horse rumps crop the grass,

a chestnut and a pale white one,
tough fur steaming in winter sun.

To want little more than these
dark-cleaved flanks beneath shaded trees.

The Canoe

Webbing gone, mattress dipped
to the ground – single kayak,
meandering on night's tributaries.
We've rocked in your deep belly now,
two dreams pressed into the shape of one.

Think of the dark water, blue water
with the curtains closed. Think
of the creak of the canvas and wood.
Think of the small silver fish,
like moonlight, like starlight

shattered at our mouths and our lips.
Think of us shooting the rapids,
tumbling into the foam.
Think of us, think of us then love,
riding the turtleback home.

Leaving and Remaining

If you must go then leave me
simple things I know –
sea-blue mussel, shell of crab,
pin on me a crusted starfish
like the King of Norway had.

Leave me your familiar things
to lie within, letters, books
and rings that you have touched
and looked on, that somehow
when I pick them up still

speak and smell to me of you –
a jumper or a frock will do.
Leave me a box
to put these things in
and I will be a rock for you

the sea has crawled within.
I'd like an abacus too,
on a soft wood frame to sing
the days on, while I am here
alone and you are gone.

Wound

Your hair lies wound in my comb
now you've gone home.
I touch the sink where you leant
to right yourself before you went.

The mirror shows my eyes now
where your eyes were, eyebrows,
lips, semblance of your mouth and hair.
Its faint shadows absorb me there.

You leave me and Billy Holliday sings.
You leave something in these things,
lipstick-lips on the white cup rim,
coffee smell and your scent lingering.

In my hands, sat again in my chair,
I curl two strands of your long brown hair.
I never dreamt the pain of this love's hell.
To stay together, loving, in betrayal.

Meditations on Cruelty

And does the moorhen turn all this
beneath her wing? The swan beneath her hiss
as I pass her in the park? She holds her seven

cygnets against water voles and rats and even
me. She's right to flesh her head with slaughter
pushing her hope through the shadowy water.

Lines Written in Hyde Park

This moment lives without you and with me.
It is peculiar to feel that I am alive
and it is not possible for me to see
you. How is it that separate we can live?

How is it that that betrayal we can share?
Me, I'm sitting in the middle of Hyde Park.
A man is kicking dust on a dappled grey mare,
the light around him is already growing dark

even as the horse hooves kick high and free.
So all your moments without me still exist
and your life goes on separate from me.
In so ordinary a world of dust and mist

if thought could be the very touch of love
I think this moment fully in the instant that it dies.
To you I've offered all I have to give.
I pray the thought will reach you where you lie.

15 Childhood Poems

from *Something Simple*

Accident

David was in for observation.
His face was like Carnation
milk. But they were *observing* him.
I'd observed him. He was boring.

Large green tents of clothes, gowns
and hats with people in, swished around.
They all smelt of sick.
Mum said it was carbolic. It was sick.

He'd landed in the drain on his head.
Mum had gone white, David bright red.
But there was no fracture and no crack.
And we had to have him back.

New Boy

No, I couldn't play with them at football!
until I'd sat and eaten all
their unwanted plodges of grey mashed
potato. And if I told they'd bash

my face in. Gobbling custard noise,
spoons in fists; the bully boys.
Alone, beneath my silences, the sorrow
of each hard, glutinous, sticky swallow.

Convalescent

Mellow smell of gas
popping in a room. Distant glass
with flight of bird-shadows on.
Footsteps near on stairs, then gone.

Once I knew it was school lunchtime
sickness's desolation seemed sublime.
Dug into blankets on the settee
I croaked down broth and warm weak tea.

Hidden inside my pyjamas I dreamt
of sickness so pervasive no attempt
to get me back to school could ever
be considered. I'd lie cosseted forever,

the joy of sickness in my limbs –
A sad joy, bruised inside, like hymns.

Water

I argued with my mother
on the subject of water.
Our Doctor mumbled 'sample'
and there was a clear bottle

labelled with a yellow band
he concealed into her hand.
All the way down the hill
home we argued. Right till

the front door she insisted
while I shook my head;
my water, like my shoes?
I hadn't met the idea of whose

water water was, my water or
her water, or anyone's water.
I chewed on my satchel strap.
'He wanted it from the tap.'

Her anger couldn't sway me.
'He's got his own tap hasn't he?
If it would do that water would
do.' The Doctor used our water too?

Subterranean maternal logic, always
lapping widening circles to amaze.
Water ran hissing beneath our feet,
pumping in all houses of our street.

Water could flow in the dark, up hill?
The murmuring miracle of water. Still
it was disgusting that he wanted mine.
I planned to give him turpentine.

Marred by Love

We kids had to 'get to know' the new dog.
Huge as a half-charred log,
black fur prowling a black-eared head,
she sat at the door. Dead

quiet together we didn't dare move. She
watched us, honey-eyed, watchingly,
head and ears on guard in semaphore
if we moved towards her or the door.

Dad had got her from an American
with a flat head, an Air Force policeman
who they said had to go back
to wherever he'd come from. A slack

silver chain in the fur of her coat
she'd growled in the depths of her throat,
as his toecaps said goodbye in the hall.
He'd turned and given another call.

She'd sat her huge head, eyes intent
to his leg. He'd thrumped her fur. Obedient,
trained for him she'd never guard
another leg or boot or gun. Marred

by love she was a one-man dog.
Her mouth a mesh of snapping cogs,
white as she lolled her tongue,
she'd die unless we gave her love a home.

Flesh like holsters snapped along her gums.
We watched her stomach beating like drums
and pretended at cards on the dining
table as she barked then lay her whining

muzzle whimpering on her paws. Outside
the song of his car engine died.
She'd love us this way Gran and Pop said,
the shotgun of her nostrils at our heads.

Incident at Southend-on-Sea

Yacht sails in the estuary of cold, grey sea
skimming their white fins free to Tilbury,
Sheerness gleaming like oil, and Gravesend
– a dark glimmer of cranes at the far end
of what the eye could see. Here, gleaming over mud,

the sea renewed itself in a skin of soft soapy suds.
The long mud had drawn us out like wading gulls,
to seek worms in the worm holes, poke fish skulls,
until, looking back, we saw no more acres of dark
land behind us, only thick sea in a black prowling arc,

ridged with shark fins. 'The tide's turned,' Mum said.
'It's come in behind us. We've got to head
back. Now!' Mum smiled into David's cornflower eyes.
The waters surging through her large thighs
Gran gripped onto mine and Pat's hands

but brown water pulled her down into the mud-sand
and waves of frothy oil-foam plunged over
her head, drowning her mouth and hair. In seaweed-covered
serpents, in greedy salt water she lay, no sound
but a moan capable from her mouth. Dark pound

I heard, thrashing in my ears of the jealous sea,
starving for our flesh, for Pat, David, hungry for me.
'Run' Mum said, 'run!' And we ran through the waves,
water rising up in toothless mouths. Hungry black caves
I just stood and stared into. 'Go on!' Gran

slipped again and jerked at my hand.
I looked down into her eyes as she snatched me near
and there I saw it – the dark gaping dread of her fear.
The Gods could not protect us from darkness I saw.
We all lay gasping, spewed onto the shore.

Ode to the West Wind

'Will ye not come home brother?'
I said, poetic with sadness, to my grandmother's
face as she put a plate of beans on toast steaming
in front of me. I cradled my Byronic face. Dreaming

out of school, past garages and shops the poem
had rolled me like a river of magic home;
'Song to a man's soul, brother, fire to a man's brain,
To hear the wild seas and see the merry spring again.'

'What's he talking about? What's he going on about?'
Gran asked. Mum said 'Eat it while it's hot.'
My heart sprang over the table. 'Ye have long been away.
It's April, and blossom time, and white is the May.'

Dad knocked me one, and put his pipe on the mantel shelf.
My blossoming heart spread inwards, inside myself,
Pop belched, Gran pared skin off her bunioned feet.
'It's a poem,' Pat's tomato mouth said, 'He's learning it

for school.' 'Poem? Wants something doesn't he?'
Light shone on the cured ham bone of Gran's peevish knee,
'What's he learning a poem for? The little fool.'
Next day my heart fluttered at the windows of the school –

"It's the white road westwards is the road I must tread
To the green grass, cool grass, and rest for heart and head,
To the violets and the warm hearts and the thrushes' song,
In the fine land, the west land, the land where I belong."

In Darkness

Safe again in our old clothes
we met in dunkey rhubarb, dog rose
and blackberry up on the hill
behind the police station, the smell

and shape of our old jeans welcoming us.
Tussling in hillocks of mattocky grass
we lay looking over the edge
of the mine shaft – the ledge on ledge

of stones and flints and daisies
where the turf fell away. Our knees
clattered pebbles down into the deep
turquoise silence; the stony, steep

sides singing them away into nothing,
a long, drawn silence of nothing. Dingling
out of the nettles, bees and dark midges
numbed round the wild blackberry hedges

and the blue eye of the mine shaft shone
like a milk of magnesia bottle in sun.
Pillows of white clouds drifted across it.
We held each other down, sat

with knees pinning our arms to the sides
of our heads and thought we'd hide
up here and never go to school again.
Leave them calling out our names

into the wet dusk misting over
the lost mine. Lying in grasses and clover
feeding on blackberries and clear spring
water, in darkness we'd sing.

Handstands for Pamela

Pamela's mother had a large blue eye,
blue as a milk of magnesia bottle. I
feared her skin, like a walnut round her chin,

her legs pink and surgical and thin,
and her smell, like her house – Methodism;
but I stared at that glass prism,

sightlessly piercing me right through.
I wanted Pamela but The Eye was there too.
Pamela was three years older than me.

Wonderful looking she sat shelling peas,
chatting and nodding to people coming
up and down their stony road, humming,

singing and calling out loud, 'Hello
my 'andsome.' I lived stupid and slow
in the scent of her pea-podding hands.

I stole her daisies. I gave handstands
that she and Blue Eye applauded.
Pamela kissed my forehead.

The Plume of Feathers

John Tedray didn't have a mother;
he had a barmaid. In *The Plume of Feathers*,

with bottle-glass doors and men
throbbing in the dark and an ivy garden,

she kept hundreds of miners in the dark,
made them drink brown mine water. To embark

onto that slippery sea of beery noise
was forbidden for us peering boys,

so we gathered all the glasses we could find
from the tables and benches and lined

them up beneath the hammock and apple trees.
Legs out, sailors on hot African seas,

all of us in its belly, squashed in the wind,
with hot wasps bursting fat apple skins,

we lay waiting as she paddled the long grasses,
humming shepherdess of all stray glasses.

Bare heels sucking her shoes, she wore light
floaty blouses gifting her bosoms apple-white.

We dived deep into the drowning as she bent
down, tumbling from the hammock as we leant

too far. Naked heels sucking her away,
breaking the daisy foam swam Mrs Tedray.

Sunday People

The car boot burst hot car-smell and sand
when we opened it, arms and hands
full of things: cricket stumps, big radio,
bags of sandwiches, flasks of tea, the lilos
rippling like Pat's rubbery swimsuit, half full
of air. I bounced the bounce bouncing ball,
listening to the sound change as it went higher.
Towels and bags round the jack and spare tyre,

Dad drove us to the church gate. He
sat in the car up the road, radio on, and we
mumbled Holy Mass inside the dark
mosaic of stained glass windows lit with sparks
of gold from chalices and candles – marble floor,
mumbling feet, aching knees, creaking door.
Outside as he drove the car smelt of tobacco. He
had the *News of the World* on his knees

and print like Ash Wednesday on his brow. His pipe
sang to us out the window. 'I gave her a good wipe
over with the shammy. Got the midges and flies
off.' On my clothes I smelt the Misereres
clinging. A photo in the paper lurked black as murder –
a girl, bare breasted, 'The day he killed her.'
Dad swung all the windows open as we drove.
The sun was like the Eucharist. The earth wore mauve.

Victory and Defeat

Sir's face on the Evening News. Recalled
at the age of thirty one! For Cornwall.
To burly at Gloucester for the Cornish pack.

His broken nose said he was glad to be back.
I cheered the Cornish jerseys running away,
yelled for distant hours as they stayed

away from where I was on the grass,
till suddenly, large legs blundered past.
In the gathering gloom and dusk of Redruth,

in smell of mackintoshes and wet earth,
I watched the mud-backs of the men
thunder each other to the grass, then

pile like lowing cattle, mud-heads in a mound
of steam and rain, heels mauling the ground.
And I stood blurred in the roar, loud

for Cornwall, for Sir. Modest and proud.
The stand lights spiralling, I turned and ran
through throngs of overcoats, macs and hats. A man

held a boy aloft, his arms like a tree on the coast,
and the stand lights melted like butter on toast.
And I was out there on the magic pitch,

and it was just grass, earth like in a ditch.
Just grass and earth, ordinary as air.
Rain wet its stanchions of stars in my hair.

He was bent above me, all sweat and mud–
bludgeoned. His nose a rosette of dried blood.
His shoulders were smaller. Sunk in his caked

and lined face I saw in his eyes a vast ache.
I gabbled, sad, 'I saw you give that diving pass.
We won, didn't we?' His shadow limped on past.

Beach Cricket

On the wet sand we played cricket,
two piles of stones as wickets.
Mum caught and bowled Dad and giggled.
Pat danced and drew squiggles
with her heels in the sand,
then walked about in a handstand

looking back to see where she'd
been, and fell over, knock-kneed.
Mum stuck her tongue out, clenched
between her lips, while she wrenched
the ball away from her into the air.
'Oh no,' she said, 'it's not fair.'

And flung the bat down as Dad
caught it. 'Out! You're out,' Dad said,
laughing finger raised. My turn to bat.
Dad bowled me his quick one, fast and flat.
'Not too fast.' 'Okay, here's my yorker
instead.' Their laughter was raucous

as the ball plopped at my feet. 'Googly
next.' I swung the bat emptily.
Upside down Pat's bare feet applauded.
'Now my Chinaman,' Dad's devious arm said.
In quivering air the spinning ball hung
a parabola of water towards me. I swung

out with the bat, both eyes shut.
In my darkness I heard a sodden splat
and looking up, the ball up high, plopped
into a slumbering rock pool. Pat had to hop
up for it. I ran twenty-eight.
He never taught me to play straight.

Radio-Heroes

Tumultuous in the Co-op they autographed my book
next to Auntie Doris's 'By hook or by crook.'
I watched them write *Richie Benaud*, *Wally Grout*
and stared at their chins to hear them shout

'Owzat?!' But they didn't. They autographed
pale yellow bats, with hairy hands, and laughed
in strange accents. Big-nosed, they were the *Aussies*.
Alan Davidson, he wrote. *Graham McKenzie*.

Their big shoulders freckled their scrawl,
Neil Harvey, *Bill Lawry*, *Norman O'Neill*,
into my red autograph book. I traced the curves.
They wrote as they bowled, with swing and swerve.

Surprised, I thought *Aussies* were human,
in blazers. Men like my Dad. Not like 'Trueman,'
when Dad said it, or 'Here comes Fiery Fred',
the radio growled, 'black hair flopping on his head.'

Some Notes

The author is grateful to Thames & Hudson Ltd for permission to quote, on p24, from *The Poet's Manual and Rhyming Dictionary* by Frances Stillman. Also to William Heinemann Ltd for permission to quote, on p45, from *Ode To The West Wind* by John Masefield.

The Italian quotation on p16 roughly translates as 'the study of painting is hard while the sea grows ever wilder.'